# DEEP STATE DEFECTOR VI

# DEEP STATE DEFECTOR VI

Rahul Dev Manchanda, Esq

Copyright © 2023 by Rahul Dev Manchanda, Esq.

Library of Congress Control Number: 2019920561
ISBN: Softcover 979-8-3694-0506-2
eBook 979-8-3694-0505-5

All rights reserved. No part of this book may be reproduced or transmitted in any form or by any means, electronic or mechanical, including photocopying, recording, or by any information storage and retrieval system, without permission in writing from the copyright owner.

Any people depicted in stock imagery provided by Getty Images are models, and such images are being used for illustrative purposes only. Certain stock imagery © Getty Images.

Print information available on the last page.

Rev. date: 08/21/2023

To order additional copies of this book, contact:
Xlibris
844-714-8691
www.Xlibris.com
Orders@Xlibris.com
855211

# Contents

| | | |
|---|---|---|
| Chapter 1 | The Unbearable Heaviness Of Being A CEO | 1 |
| Chapter 2 | Let's Face It - America's Southern Border Is An Invasion And War Being Waged By Its Enemies | 5 |
| Chapter 3 | America Is Only As "Exceptional" As The "Leaders" Running It | 8 |
| Chapter 4 | The Migrant Crises All Over The World Are Just Reactions To Centuries Long Exploitation and Oppression By The Wealthy Nations Run By Their Oligarch Family Ancestors | 11 |
| Chapter 5 | American Law Is An Illusion | 13 |
| Chapter 6 | When Did Americans Become So Squeamish? | 15 |
| Chapter 7 | The Problem Is That The Lawbreakers Have The National Security Letters | 18 |
| Chapter 8 | The Return Of The Agent Provocateur | 22 |
| Chapter 9 | The Evolving "Keiretsu" Of The American Banking System | 26 |
| Chapter 10 | Time To Investigate The Inspector Generals | 29 |
| Chapter 11 | America Can Learn A Lot From Other Countries | 31 |
| Chapter 12 | Variety Is The Spice Of Life, But Extremism Is The Mouth That Burns | 33 |
| Chapter 13 | American Small Business Getting Crushed By Big Corporations And Government Funded Competitors | 35 |
| Chapter 14 | Big Tech Payment Systems Are Slowly Replacing The American Judiciary | 37 |
| Chapter 15 | Organized Jews Are Planning To Leave America To Organized Blacks | 39 |

Chapter 16  Global Communists And Global Oligarchs Have Made Civil Rights Violations Out Of Lifestyle Choices ........................................................................ 41

Chapter 17  Humanity Needs To Ensure That Artificial Intelligence Is Also Programmed By Humanists, Not Just Control Freaks, Oligarchs, and Sociopaths ... 44

Chapter 18  Marjorie Taylor Greene Has Bigger Balls Than All Of Her Republican Male Colleagues Combined ......... 46

Chapter 19  Rothschild's Affirmative Action Program ........................ 48

Chapter 20  The Use Of The Word "Woke" To Describe Annoying Abusers Of Equity Is The Ultimate Gaslight By The Deep State Oligarchy/Communists ... 51

# Chapter 1

## *The Unbearable Heaviness Of Being A CEO*

*"No one knows what it's like, to be the bad man, to be the sad man, behind blue eyes. No one knows what it's like, to be hated, to be fated."*

— Behind Blue Eyes, The WHO (1971).

The trend these days, especially when the world is closing upon itself and becoming more interlinked via the internet, fiber optics, lightning fast air and ground travel, facsimiles and emails, text messages and cellular connectivity, is that the masses of the world are talking, from all walks of life, religions, races, cultures, countries, sexes, genders and age groups, to share their notes and commiserate about how much their lives suck and why it sucks - and invariably, the blame is always laid at the feet of the individual or entity that provides them money or capital or food or sustenance, so that they can live, pay bills, pay their rent or housing costs, provide themselves medical care, or take care of their children and families.

If they had tried to start a business or became self-employed, and failed at this, then their anger is even more pronounced, sharp and unstable.

With the advent of this now more closely connected human species on planet earth, there was first a general societal and world cultural movement to first, throw off any monarchies that stayed in existence as they were thought to be remnants of the oppressive but undeserved hereditary emperors and czars of the past, ruling over historical geographical entities and tracts of land scattered throughout most of the world, usually punctuated and synonymous with imposed order backed up by organized and institutionalized cruelty, violence, abuse (physical, mental, sexual, psychological, emotional), racism, sexism, discrimination, colonialism, exploitation, oppression, outright theft, over-taxation, fear, incarceration, or even worse, the "punishment" of death.

These are obviously horrific memories, but still carried within the DNA and oral and literary record of the millennia-plus historically oppressed, and memories passed down from generation to generation, usually while the teller and listener shudder with spine and nerve tingling anxiety and physical revulsion, "never to be repeated again," they always reiterate.

So the world's collective post-traumatic stress disorder world has quickly become a "workers of the world unite" paradise, wherein even on Tik Tok and other social media, young Generation Z (children) make videos and tout the benefits of such destructive and company destroying/sabotaging acts as "ghosting, "quiet quitting," "zero notice," or other such methods of sociopathically, irresponsibly simply walking out of a job or business, without any remorse or concern for their customers, clients, colleagues, vendors, contractors, and most certainly, their BOSS.

Because that BOSS is a bad word, a bad person, as we are all trained to believe and think, as they are the inheritors of the mantle of the cruel, blood thirsty, arbitrary, and capricious "emperors" of the past, who according to them, deserve nothing but mass murder such as the one that was inflicted and imposed on the Czar and Czarina of Russia and his children when the Communists/Leninists took over the Russian Empire in the October Revolution of 1917.

Of course, this is a sick, twisted, counterproductive, and self-boomeranging act because ultimately, if you kill the proverbial "golden goose" that provides food, housing, medical care, nourishment, security, and money, then you are literally killing yourself and your family.

So the world is now at the precipice, in a transition moment, where we are struggling to grapple with, and find balance by and between the CEOs and Business Owners of the world, and their far greater in number Workers of the World, so that both sides can be happy and well adjusted, as both sides need each other as much as possible.

This therefore will necessarily involve some new rules and regulations that also favor CEOs, Business Owners, and Bosses, because for the past 75 years (and possibly 100 plus years since the Russian Communist Revolution), things have gone really badly for business owners and their rights.

Not every CEO or business owner makes millions or billions per year, in fact, statistics show that the vast majority of business owners and CEOs of companies sometimes make even less money per year than their own prized employees, only they are forced to constantly deal with the Communist-inspired legacies of CEO whippings and regulation, such as severe and constant attacks from local and federal departments of taxation, labor departments, ethics departments, different political parties and ideologues, political corruption, favored competition due to corruption, online internet slander and defamation, sabotage from others, frivolous investigations from too many regulatory agencies/bodies, inflation, currency and monetary manipulation from the Federal Reserve, employee illness (or faked illness), paid maternity and family leave, massively skyrocketing "minimum wage" requirements imposed on their wallets, near immunity from liability when fraudster employees "hit and run" their companies with false claims of a "hostile work environment" or some other cover to justify their incompetence or evil acts, no sympathy from society or judges or legislatures, and other such slings and arrows of outrageous fortune being hurled at them, 24 hours a day, 7 days a week, 365 days per year, rain or shine, while their employees generally enjoy a 40 hour work week lying on a hammock drinking a mint julep on the weekends, with **<u>NONE</u>** of those attacks.

It's time to re-evaluate, and for CEOs and Business Owners to also stand up, assert their own rights, and demand a "correcting of the market" when it comes to their own rights and undue burdens placed upon them, not just because it is the right thing to do (see Ayn Ran, <u>Atlas Shrugged</u>) but also because the world, literally depends upon it.

If there are no CEOs, no business owners, or they are tortured, regulated, scrutinized, and harassed out of existence, then there are no jobs, no taxes paid, no money for workers, and therefore no food, security, housing, medical care for employees (who enjoy those weekend mint juleps while lying in their hammocks) or their families and children.

Government certainly cannot step into the breach to provide these things, as the last 100 years of communist and socialist failure, year after year, country after country, continent after continent, have proven this, beyond a reasonable doubt.

So instead of constantly creating national holidays for "Workers' Rights," or "Secretary Day," or whatever, let's also try and collectively demand a "CEO Day," and for once in a few hundred years, give thanks and praise for those few, courageous, ingenious, hardworking, tough, resilient, creative, and generous souls who have devoted their lives to building the American (and global dream) that is their company/business, while finding the extra time, capital, and resources, to also take care of the majority of the people around them, society, and their employees (and in turn, their families and children).

# Chapter 2

## *Let's Face It – America's Southern Border Is An Invasion And War Being Waged By Its Enemies*

The above title is self-evident - there can no longer be any question about it, especially as the news, data, and facts comes in from Customs and Border officers, southwestern state government leaders, local police officers, and especially private citizens from that ground zero, as well as the reverberations from all around the United States that peoples' children, teenagers, siblings and friends are succumbing to fentanyl-laced recreational narcotics death, for absolutely no reason other than to kill them.

Other research indicates and traces this manufactured fentanyl directly to nation states and countries that are at war with America, either through economics and trade, or through downright traditional bullets, tanks, airplanes and guns.

Let there be no mistake, the United States of America is under a "boiling frog" attack, sort of like Pearl Harbor in slow motion, so that the People won't wake up to it, until it is too late.

Perhaps that's what the billions of dollars to Joe Biden and his family bought?

An end and a final destruction to the United States of America as we know it, and precision-guided by foreign born Cuban traitor DHS Chief

Alejandro Mayorkas leading the charge, who might as well be the cigar-chomping Fidel Castro opening our gates just like he did with the Mariel criminal refugee crisis back in the 1980s, wherein Cuba emptied all of its jails of the most dangerous, crazy, violent and drug addicted prisoners and sent them to Florida on countless boats, kind of like a satanic version of Christopher Columbus' Nina, Pinta, and Santa Maria commissioned by Queen Isabella and King Ferdinand of Spain back in 1492.

All of the previously ignored "rednecks" and "racists" on the southern border have now been proven to be correct, and have been replaced in the public eye by latin immigration officers and police, as well as a recent visit down to the border by New York City Mayor Eric Adams just to demonstrate to the world (and the United Nations Human Rights Council) that this is **_NOT_** a racial issue, as they tried to pin on former President Donald Trump, or on Texas Governor Gregory Abbot or his faithful Attorney General Ken Paxton, but rather a race, color, religious and ethnically blind NATIONAL SECURITY ISSUE.

People are dying, left and right, in the millions, from all walks of life, all races and religions, all sexes, and all "gender pronouns."

Fentanyl and cartel automatic weapons and machetes do not discriminate, and are only concerned with amassing as much of the green backs of the United States to pump back into their 5 main cartel leaders ruling Mexico, but now splintering and branching out, sometimes calling themselves Michoacan, Knights Templar, La Familia, Tijuana, Jalisco New Generation, Beltran Leyva, Sinaloa, Medellin, Gulf, Los Zetas, and Juarez Cartel.

While the enemies of America both inside and out decry and defame Congresswomen Marjorie Taylor Greene, she seems to be the only one who gets it - perhaps that's why her enemies are so well funded - with coke money.

Whoever said "a little coke money don't hurt nobody" was wrong about the American southern border, and Congresswoman Greene's call for paramilitary retaliation, bombing, air raids, hit squads, even standing armies need to now be voted on and consented to by the American Congress and U.S. Senate immediately - but unfortunately 90% of those "elected leaders" are riding high and re-elected to office DIRECTLY BY THE MONEY COMING FROM THOSE CARTELS.

The American people, their children and families, are currently being held hostage while their elected leaders like Nancy Pelosi live behind gates communities and having more security than the most famous Hollywood celebrities, while the American people are totally naked and exposed, inundated daily by gang wars, cartel wars, getting shot in the streets, having their homes invaded and cars stolen as far north as Westchester County New York, where these "migrants" then immediately become the "foot soldiers" and "cheap labor" and "tips of the tentacles" of these various and violent Mexican drug cartels in terms of illicit narcotics and weapons distribution, murder, terrorism, crime and rape.

The American people need to demand that their Congress and Senate take immediate military action with the (hopeful) consent of the Executive Branch, otherwise this looks like it will result in a re-heated version of the Battle of the Alamo of 1836 or even the much greater Spanish-American War of 1898.

If America's elected leaders don't take the necessary military action that their citizenry demands, then they should not be surprised if those same American voters take matters into their own hands, with organized militia and enclaves, in order to defend their life, liberty and property, as only they know how.

# CHAPTER 3

## *America Is Only As "Exceptional" As The "Leaders" Running It*

Undersigned author can not be the only American who is sick to the back teeth of hearing the phrase, over and over, that "America is exceptional," by the same self-congratulatory thieves who are robbing, fleecing, and exploiting it, and its people.

As Samuel Johnson said on April 7, 1775, "Patriotism is the last refuge of the scoundrel," and nowhere is that more apparent than in today's American politics, whether Republican or Democrat, conservative or liberal.

The fact remains that America is only as great as the leaders that run it, and right now, those leaders are extremely UN-exceptional.

We have incompetents, corrupt, and lazy bureaucrats inhabiting all 3 branches of the U.S. Government, including the judiciary, executive and legislative who are more interested in window dressing and how they appear on their 5 minute sound bites on Fox News, CNN, or MSNBC, rather than what they actually accomplish on the record, for the American people.

Meanwhile, after these lying thieves and creeps have finished their sound bites for the camera, they seemingly turn around, go back into their nice luxurious offices near the Capitol or Rotunda building, and start accepting and cashing massive "lobbying" (see bribery) checks from countless special interest and anti-American entities hell-bent on undermining the United States Constitution and further hanging out the American people to dry.

Queen Gertrude in Shakespeare's Hamlet said that "the lady doth protest too much," which is a pretty good indication that the louder the voice in the senate or congress, the less that those people actually do in private, sounding their screams like a clarion call into the halls of the legislature so that the rich wealthy entities that they scream at, will miraculously appear bearing gifts and cash in order to shut them up (at least until the next election cycle).

This is really no difference that a low end, street level, "protection racket" which the dirty street mobs of New York City and other major cities perfected since the time of this country's founding (see, Tammany Hall, and Boss Tweed).

One only has to scan the latest YouTube sound bites each week to see small "feature films" lasting only a few minutes, wherein these inept bullshitters in congress and the senate appear to be tearing a new hole into one of their latest wealthy human sacrificial lambs, but then immediately rise and leave the room when the cameras move on to the next pickpocket politician.

Names like Ted Cruz, Josh Hawley, John Kennedy, Matt Gaetz, Jim Jordan, Lindsey Graham, Ilhan Omar, Alexandria Ocasio Cortez, Rand Paul, John Cornyn, Lauren Boebert, Ron Johnson, Marsha Blackburn, Marco Rubio, Tom Cotton, Chuck Schumer, Jerrold Nadler, Bernie Sanders, Elizabeth Warren, Mitch McConnell and many other political prostitutes appear like baseball cards in this bullshit circus every day (no political party is better, or worse, than the other in this regard, because they all work for the same oligarchs/plutocrats).

These elected grand standers then fully expect that their telephones will then ring and be answered by their lovely receptionists, with, guess who?

A humble bowing representative bearings gifts and cash from the poor hapless shakedown recipient that they were just yelling at, a few minutes ago, on camera.

In comes the cash, and the reciprocal promises by that politician to "shut down" any current investigations, or to "sabotage" any upcoming indictments or prosecutions, etc with a "phone call' or some other bullying mechanism.

And so it goes, day in day out, while the American debt blossoms like a mushroom cloud on the horizon, yesterday 22 trillion, tomorrow 33 trillion, and then some, while the rich get richer, the middle class disappears, and the poor get poorer (and die).

# Chapter 4

## *The Migrant Crises All Over The World Are Just Reactions To Centuries Long Exploitation and Oppression By The Wealthy Nations Run By Their Oligarch Family Ancestors*

The vast majority of the major oligarch wealthy families in Europe and the West are still ancestry oligarchical families whose grandparents, if not great-great grandparents, colonized, exploited, oppressed, stole, and murdered the indigenous people whom they now desperately try and keep out of their nations with the use (and abuse) of unconstitutional/non-humanitarian terrorism laws, immigration laws, and other criminal laws designed to stem the rising tide of the karmically angry, downtrodden, and poverty stricken migrants who are pouring over the borders all over the world into the wealthy nations.

While these hypocritical Oligarchs and Plutocrats tend to curse and hate men like billionaire activist George Soros, who are instrumental in using their billions of dollars to streamline and guide these migrants with well-paid lawyers and activists into these invaded nations, one must never lose sight of the fact that the trillions of dollars in infrastructure, wealth and oligarch/plutocrat wealth can be linearly and directly traced to the mountains, gold mines, silver mines, precious stones mines, fields, and other raw materials of the countries that have now been left naked and barren from the centuries long plundering, raping, and theft by the nations that are now keeping these migrant people away from their own wealth.

Additionally, the only migrants that these nations allow into the USA are those that can somehow become "useful" to the oligarchs/plutocrats that be, whether in the form of cheap or unskilled labor, or at best, traitors to their left behind people and nations, in order to become spies, turncoats, media talking heads, and "think tank" members who can use their innate knowledge of these "enemy countries" (according to the oligarchs/plutocrats) to further smash those already assaulted and raped countries into dust.

If these migrants do not turn out to become useful to the admitting wealthy nations, then those oligarchs/plutocrats will force and push their own law enforcement, military, intelligence services, media, legislators, judiciary and executive branches to enact laws and situations which are designed explicitly to incarcerate, deport, marginalize, kill, murder, rape, destabilize, disorient, and destroy those newly arrived immigrants until they can no longer fight or resist the blood thirsty foreign and domestic policies originated in the boardrooms (and country clubs) of the oligarchs and plutocrats.

In many ways, the phrase "chickens coming home to roost" is an apt and fitting way to describe this process, but the unfortunate part is that none of the original thieves and criminals (or their currently living oligarch ancestors) pay any price for this migrant crisis, as they are all safe and sound and neatly locked behind gated communities in media-hidden cities and locales scattered all throughout the world, and kept out of the major media because, well, they either own the media, or are fellow club members of those who own the media.

The only ones who suffer are those people on the ground, i.e., the middle class and poor invaded, and the invaders, who do battle on the streets and suffer and die while the wealthy oligarchs and plutocrats sip champagne, smoke expensive cigars, and feast on caviar in their billion dollar enclaves.

# Chapter 5

## *American Law Is An Illusion*

The problem with America, its critics say, is that "everything is for sale."

That there is no moral compass, no moral guidance, and no reverence of God existing in the United States at the top-most levels of government, anymore (whether executive, judiciary, or legislative).

This means that we have become a nation with a government of Luciferians, or "light-seekers," it seems, those who only "seek the truth," or whatever that means.

Many argue that it all started with some of the Founding Fathers, who they described as "deists," that is, those who believe that while God (or Providence) with his natural laws, may have created the world, but that He somehow walked away from this creation, and left it in the hands of humanity's "betters," i.e., those illuminated and educated (and fit) to rule the world and its people, in his stead.

The problem is, that these "betters" are after all, only human, and are susceptible to all of the temptations that have plagued humanity since time immemorial - money, sex, pleasure, greed, avarice, lust, anger, etc - to the point that where everyone, it seems, has a "price."

And in America, where everything is for sale, that also includes its "leaders."

And these leaders also include its lawmakers, its judges, and its executors.

*Ergo*, the more money that you have to purchase and buy America's leaders' loyalty and action, the more likely that you will sway the American "legal system" to your own ends and desires.

Now that the illusion of the God-head has been forcibly stripped away from the fabric of American society, wherein there is open Satanism (a devolution of Luciferianism or Deism), there is no longer even an *attempt* by American (and global) oligarchs to even "pretend" or "feign" that there is a legitimate, non-corrupted American legal system.

It is strictly run by money, lobbying power (see bribery), outright thievery, and corruption.

Even the FBI and DOJ, if not the stasi-like DHS, have been politicized by whomever holds the financial purse strings of America's politicians, leaders, lawmakers, judges and executors at any given moment.

Of course, the main stream corporate owned media, always follows the money power as well.

And any competing media entity (usually foreign) is quickly banned or marginalized as "fake news" at best, or "foreign espionage propaganda," at worst, subject to all sorts of criminal investigation and prosecution.

This is of course, all going to plan, as per America's oligarchy and plutocracy.

And the proverbial noose around the average Americans' collective necks, is getting tighter, and tighter.

The boiling frog of American freedom is now nearly complete, and will only take one or two more "false flags" for the heavy hand of complete and total totalitarianism to fall like the iron curtain that it actually is, this time, encircling the entire globe in its suffocating cloak.

Enjoy your freedom while you can, for the End of that Freedom, is Nigh.

# Chapter 6

## *When Did Americans Become So Squeamish?*

It used to be, judging from those little time capsules known as movies and motion pictures, that Americans used to be a brave, tough, and resilient lot, with thick skin and an even thicker sense of self-confidence.

Americans were known the world over for being brash, bold and even boorish at times.

Think of one our greatest American Presidents, Theodore "Teddy" Roosevelt, who epitomized the American wild west, even though he was born and came into money, he fought long and hard to shed that image.

Teddy Roosevelt later became what Vladimir Putin has become today on the global stage, a bare-chested half man, half animal, with the suave smooth sophistication to also know how to put on a good suit.

Even the iconic James Bond characters have become more lukewarm and soft, coming all the way down from Sean Connery's gritty (if not almost criminal) mannerisms and behavior, then lilting by the increasingly effeminate Roger Moore, and then landing at the all around pretty Pierce Brosnan, who was then finally replaced by the ruggedly ugly Daniel Craig, kind of like how James Bond always seemed to pull up his crashing plane before hitting the cliffs.

Well, at least the British get it.

And this is also probably one of the reasons that the British Monarchy always makes sure that their sons serve in the military - the Royal Air Force or whatever, in order to go through that man-making rite of passage as even the Native American Indians used to put their prepubescent children through, often banishing them for a few weeks or months to live out in the wild, cold, hungry, scared and alone, until what came back was either dead, or hard as nails.

Because life is hard, and survival is hard.

We lose sight of that reality in a soft and tepid society where no one really is worried about where their next meal is coming from, whether from their parents, their schools, or the nearest soup kitchen, or worst of all, jail.

But there still are people starving in this world, in the poorer parts of the world, where they would pray for a stale peanut butter and jelly sandwich from their local penitentiary.

Unfortunately, this is also part and parcel of the American working world, where employee rights have gone so high that now, that to even swear in front of another employee if one stubs their toe, theoretically creates a "hostile working environment," where the communist infiltrators at the local Department of Labor (mostly New York City) jot that down and use it to shovel free taxpayer money at the eternally slovenly, lazy, and miscreant "quiet quitters" of the modern millennial age.

Gone are the self starters, the bullet biters, and the lift yourself up by the britches type of American in corporate and mainstream America.

Part of the blame can fall on the globalized society of today, where the soft handed, lotion using Europeans have come over to the Americas in droves, looking for jobs and easy sex, as their economies stagnate and tank due to the lack of the aforementioned grit, ingenuity, and creators of American industry and technology.

Even American bankers and financial professionals have a much fouler tongue than their European or other older civilization counterparts, which are always dominated by generationally wealthy soft handed well educated professionals.

So let's not lose our American Pioneer Spirit, or the Wild Wild West that used to punctuate our every step and move in today's reluctantly globalized America - because at the end of the day, that's what made America great in the first place.

Not "polite English."

# Chapter 7

## *The Problem Is That The Lawbreakers Have The National Security Letters*

You don't have to be a rocket scientist to deduce that it always seems that whenever massive criminal investigations and matters finally reach the zenith, or the penultimate point of no return, when it seems like the vast empire of criminality and all of its evil participants are about to be exposed, shut down, arrested, charged, tried and imprisoned, that it all seems to just fall apart.

Why is that, one might ask?

Well, it's really quite simple - the rampant abuse of the National Security Letter ("NSL").

Ever major civilization has had one, or its equivalent, since time immemorial.

In the United Kingdom, our last Empire cousin, it usually comes accompanied to an esoteric law called the "Official Secrets Act."

Essentially, in the hands of its wielder, it can have devastating effects on the recipient and all of the hub and spokes within the wheel of the criminal conspiracy, large or small, real or imagined.

In effect, it is the real life equivalency of the board game Monopoly's "Get Out Of Jail Card."

This is the reason that hardly anything has happened, not even a peep, in terms of the world's massively huge criminal conspiracies and capers - from the John F. Kennedy assassination, to the Jeffrey Epstein underage sex blackmail scandal of the planet's most powerful private and public individuals, to Big Tech's totally illegal and unethical joinder with the federal governments of not only the United States but all other global governments to manipulate and control their people, etc.

In fact, there is probably not one massive global criminal enterprise that has not had countless NSLs thrown around by unscrupulous, corner-cutting, corrupt, and evil government actors since the beginning of time.

It probably was even used in the "Jack The Ripper" case all the way back to Whitechapel England, when it was discovered that the horrible murderer/rapist was in fact one of the most "connected" and powerful men in England, at the time (various conspiracies have emerged).

What exactly is a "National Security Letter?"

Well Wikipedia describes it generically as "an administrative subpoena issued by the United States government to gather information for national security purposes. NSLs do not require prior approval from a judge...NSLs typically contain a nondisclosure requirement forbidding the recipient of an NSL from disclosing the FBI had requested the information. The nondisclosure provision must be authorized by the Director of the FBI, and only after he or she certifies 'that otherwise there may result a danger to the national security of the United States; interference with a criminal, counterterrorism, or counterintelligence investigation; interference with diplomatic relations; or danger to the life or physical safety of any person.'"

The bland article goes on to discuss how the "recipient" may be able to "challenge the nondisclosure provision in federal court," but everyone and their mother knows that this is complete and total bullshit.

Any and all state or federal judges, upon receiving one of these documents, is immediately struck with terror and fear since it did not even require a judge to be issued in the first place, and is in essence therefore an "extra-judicial" document, essentially making the demand or request, "above the law," capable of even rolling up the reviewing judge into a 6 foot by 6 foot prison cell.

That is a very powerful weapon or document in the hands of a megalomaniac, sociopath, or other garden-variety criminal (which there are thousands) within the federal government.

The problem is, the record of the world is replete with countless and bottomless examples of the most hideous and brain-scrambled criminals inhabiting the highest offices of the land, such as Adolph Hitler, Pol Pot, Stalin, Mussolini, Markus Wolfe, Lavrenty Beria, and the list goes on, and on, and on.

These "government leaders" were responsible for the deaths (murders), sexual assaults, rapes, exploitation, abuse, manipulation, and other horrid crimes, in the hundreds of millions, if not billions of innocent people.

Yet, each one of them was protected by their nation's equivalent of the "National Security Letter," which immediately shut down and dismantled any type of protest, investigation, journalist, news article, questioning, public gathering, or inquiry, let alone any arrest or prosecution (or even civil lawsuit) thereon.

At many times in this country's history, various spontaneous "feeding frenzies" and "spontaneous mobs" have formed like the latest fad on the horizon, where it all seemed that this NSL phenomenon was about to unravel, taking each and every one of their users/conspirators down with them to the proverbial "hoosegow," (we all remember the FISA Court hearings, short-lived and as lasting as a firefly's ass light on a summer night) but alas, it always ended in naught.

And this, has never been an "accident" or some "logical conclusion."

This has always been about the proverbial and much discussed international "Deep State," covering up for their fellow brethren within the international "Deep State."

Or, as former President George W. Bush once said, "This is an impressive crowd. The haves and the have mores. Some people call you the elite. I call you my base."

Perhaps it is way past time for the American people, and the rest of the world, to put down their Twitter accounts (ironically the social media company where former FBI Lawyer/Agent and scumbag criminal sociopath James

Baker used his former government position to squash, quash, obfuscate, and blur the lines between private corporations and government action in order to make more money for himself, and his new employer Twitter - see GREED), I-phones and other smart phones, laptops and I-pads, and start to demand from their elected leaders, in all three branches of government (at least in the United States if not the rest of the world) to unleash, expose, undo, vitiate, and make public, each and every single National Security Letter that has ever been issued in the name of "protecting National Security."

Furthermore, according to the Wikipedia article, "like other administrative subpoenas, NSLs do not require judicial approval. For NSLs, that is because the U.S. Supreme Court has held the type of information NSLs obtain do not have a constitutionally protected reasonable expectation of privacy. The person has already provided the information to a third party, e.g., their telephone company, so they no longer have a reasonable expectation of privacy to the information and, therefore, there is no Fourth Amendment requirement to obtain court approval to obtain the information. Nonetheless, an NSL recipient may still challenge the nondisclosure provision in federal court...A media report from 2007 stated a government audit found the FBI had violated the rules more than 1,000 times in an audit of 10% of its national investigations between 2002 and 2007. Twenty such incidents involved requests by agents for information not permitted under the law... According to 2,500 pages of documents the FBI provided to the Electronic Frontier Foundation in response to a Freedom of Information Act lawsuit, the FBI had used NSLs to obtain information about individuals who were the subject of an FBI terrorism or counterintelligence investigation and information from telecommunications companies about individuals with whom the subject of the investigation had communicated. According to a September 9, 2007, New York Times report, in many cases, the target of an FBI national security letter whose records are being sought is not necessarily the actual subject of a terrorism investigation. Under the USA PATRIOT Act, the FBI must assert only that the records gathered through the letter are considered relevant to a terrorism [or counterintelligence] investigation."

So basically, anyone that someone within the Deep States hates, distrusts, doesn't like, or maybe wants to fuck his wife or girlfriend.

After all, no judge is going to either review, look at, or approve this NSL, right?

So why not.

# Chapter 8

## *The Return Of The Agent Provocateur*

Now that the United States of America has gone full blown elitist imperial totalitarian thanks to its boiling frog approach to increased but ludicrous over regulation since the end of World War 2, after all of the NAZIs and British Intelligence migrated and transformed the U.S. Intelligence and Military Industrial Complex, we see the Return of the Agent Provocateur.

Today they call her the "Karen," but in modern day parlance, that's exactly what it is.

Only it is a far more complex, deeply studied and carefully modeled tool of both law enforcement, organized crime, and all of the fascists, communists, and control freaks in between.

The Agent Provocateur only works effectively in a society where nearly everything could be construed as being illegal, and where everyone is too close for comfort, and law enforcement is literally right around the bend.

It typically takes only a few minutes, if executed effectively, to bait and switch and send an innocent man or woman into a bottomless societal jail hole for the rest of his/her natural born days.

And this concept and increased usage in every day Americana should scare the absolute shit out of you.

Wikipedia defines and describes the Agent Provocateur as "a person who commits, or who acts to entice another person to commit, an illegal or rash act or falsely implicates them in partaking in an illegal act, so as to ruin the reputation of, or entice legal action against, the target, or a group they belong to or are perceived to belong to. They may target any group, such as a peaceful protest or demonstration, a union, a political party or a company... in jurisdictions in which conspiracy is a serious crime in itself, it can be sufficient for the agent provocateur to entrap the target into discussing and planning an illegal act. It is not necessary for the illegal act to be carried out or even prepared."

We only need to see the mass arrests and incarcerations of the innocents on January 6, 2021 to see how that entire orchestrated take down by evil federal agents, law enforcement, judges, legislators, and others in the executive branch took place.

Wikipedia goes on to describe Agent Provocateurs as "may be a police officer or a secret agent of police (informant, usually a criminal with one foot in prison anyway, trying to make a deal [and lie]) who encourages suspects to carry out a crime under conditions where evidence can be obtained; or who suggests the commission of a crime to another, in hopes they will go along with the suggestion and be convicted of the crime...a political organization or government may use agents provocateurs against political opponents. The provocateurs try to incite the opponent to do counter-productive or ineffective acts to foster public disdain or provide a pretext for the final assault against the opponent...historically, labor spies, hired to infiltrate, monitor, disrupt, or subvert union activities, have used agent provocateur tactics...agent provocateur activities raise ethical and legal issues. In common law jurisdictions, the legal concept of entrapment may apply if the main impetus for the crime was the provocateur."

And since it is now common knowledge that the Federal Bureau of Investigation and the Department of Homeland Security do not exist to protect and prevent crimes against ordinary U.S. Citizens, but rather to protect "National Security," i.e., "rich folks," a.k.a. Oligarchs and Plutocrats, the American masses and their children have never been more vulnerable than they are at this point in American history.

America used to be the home of the free, land of the brave, but now it is the home of out of control Oligarchs and Plutocrats of a few thousand who have more money and power than can be counted, who are fully lording it over a veritable peasant-population of more than 350 million people.

And just like in the tyrannies of Yore, hailing back to old Europe, Asia, Africa, and the Middle East, the wealthy and connected can lop off a man's head just for looking at him cross-eyed, right here in the good old land of the USA.

Don't kid yourself and delusionally think that you are free - you are not - and it is just so very easy for an Oligarch or Plutocrat to "lose" a couple thousand dollars to pay someone to bump into you and accuse you of assault, or harass you on the street or on the internet and get you to react (FaceBook or Meta is the ultimate illustration of their use of armies of professional "community standards" leftist communist snitch losers whose job it is to "bump" into you or goad you into an off-color remark or argument, just so that you, as a "threat to the oligarchy/plutocracy" with your big mouth and truth telling ideas, can get banned for a few days, weeks, months, or even permanently), to gang stalk and harass you and your loved ones until you crack, and all the while, federal and state law enforcement not only will do absolutely **_NOTHING_** to investigate or protect you, because the odds are that the same hand and money that bought off your tormentors, have already bought them off, as well.

Nowadays, everything is a crime.

The famed criminal defense lawyer Harvey Silverglate said that the average American commits three felonies per day, from the time they wake up, to the time they go to bed (this book was written 12 years ago, and the terrain has only become worse).

And since law enforcement has no duty to protect (thank the United States Supreme Court in Town of Castle Rock v. Gonzales and its sister cases) and we are criminally over-regulated and the wealthy oligarchs in America control 99% of the wealth, it is a safe bet to say that any and all free-thinkers, political dissidents, truth tellers, whistle blowers, and other naive idiots who still believe in the United States Constitution are completely, and totally, fucked.

And this is exactly how the former Soviet Union with their Godless Communism, a nation ruled by wealthy Oligarchs and Plutocrats, killed off nearly 100 million beautiful, healthy, happy Christians, that still believed in God.

Or how Adolph Hitler, financially backed up the same international Oligarchs and Plutocrats, killed off 10 million or more innocent people in his own right.

And you can be certain that the American people are only a few years, if not months, away from that bloody purge here at home, as well.

Because those Oligarchs and Plutocrats are family run businesses and they never lost control, for the last hundreds of years, only transmitted their wealth and sick ideology down to their progeny.

The same blood purges go on today all around the world - if you are a patriot, and you love your country, and your freedom, the only thing that you can do now, is know and understand your current predicament, and be vigilant, ready, and prepared.

Because there will always be some corrupt, money hungry, greedy, soulless prick to take the seat of power in federal, state, and local law enforcement, the judiciary, the legislature, and the executive branch that the previous occupant abdicated voluntarily out of concern over violations of the U.S. Constitution, Civil Liberties, Inalienable Human Rights, and Freedom.

# Chapter 9

## *The Evolving "Keiretsu" Of The American Banking System*

The global oligarchs and banking cartels love to conduct their human rights violating experiments in all countries around the world, except for their own, such as within the United States, United Kingdom and Germany, because that's usually where these mad social scientists call home, and we all know, you don't shit where you sleep, or where others personally aggrieved by your sick and twisted social experiments can physically and legally reach you.

The socialist, discriminatory, reactionary, retaliatory, exclusionary, biased, closed off, and biased Keiretsu banking system has been a hallmark of Japanese banking as long as anyone can remember, but there was always no way that the global banking oligarchs could get away with engaging in that behavior here in the United States, which was always the common parlance.

Unfortunately, with the advent and encroachment of the new world order, where civil and human rights have already been damned since September 11, 2001 to the point of wistful memories today, all three branches of the U.S. Government have been carefully pruned and whittled out of any and all remaining patriots, courageous individuals, or honorable statesmen to speak of, replaced almost entirely by cowardly, paunchy, pudgy, dishonest, fearful, bloated, and treacherous "leaders" that populate all three branches of government, easily blown over by the faintest breath of any and all international bankers and communists who stand in their way.

As undersigned has written about before, the American financial system, like the Big Tech system, has supplanted and replaced, and in fact operates as the face of, the United States government when it comes to openly violating individual Americans' civil liberties and human rights in conducting business, transacting commerce, and otherwise trying to feed and take care of their families, employees, clients and societies if they do not "tow the line" of the sick and twisted "value systems" of the international Luciferians, who all believe that they have been given the right to rule over mankind, from birth to death, including but not limited to starving their enemies, killing them, torturing them, even depriving them of the lifeblood of cash and capital to pay their bills.

The socialist Keiretsu banking system, which really was the mainstay of the ancient Japanese samurai bushido culture adopted and then culturally appropriated by international bankers as a natural consequence and switched over to their goal of socialist control of banking and commerce, has now infiltrated and mimicked the inherent American values of private rights versus public responsibilities, only this time it has become a "terms of service" or "risk management" issue by their "underwriting departments" to talk to one another, electronically or otherwise, and to literally ban certain small businesses and individuals hated and targeted by these international bankster perverts to drive their enemies into bankruptcy and hopefully, in their minds, to either extinction or conversion, to their way of thinking.

When Barack Obama was President of the United States, they first came onto the scene with their shutting down of businesses based on "risky industries" such as guns and weapons, pornography, and other industries which on their face could be shunned by a sizable part of the U.S. population, but as everyone knows, once government is given certain powers, they never give them up, only expand them thereon.

So it should not surprise anyone, that this "power" has been expanded and broadened, to the point where any and all businesses may be deemed "risky" if that targeted business is not "liked" by the enemies of the international banker oligarchs, who could easily send multiple agent provocateurs to commit frivolous credit card charge backs or other financial attacks on that company and its merchant service accounts, or other financial attributes.

The conspiracy theorists have been claiming for decades that soon, no one will be able to buy, sell, or trade until and unless they "take the mark of the beast," well that time is nowhere clearer and closer, than now, in the present day, and it will only get worse unless these hitherto ignorant, corrupted, weak, and cowardly members of all three branches of the United States government, gets off their collective ass, and begins to both investigate, and then regulate.

# CHAPTER 10

## *Time To Investigate The Inspector Generals*

If one has spent any length of time either investigating, litigating, or complaining about unethical, illegal, immoral, or corruption behavior by any member of government, whether local, state or federal, you will find that you can go no higher in this country if each door closes, than the various Offices of the "Inspector General."

Even the Office of Special Counsel, supposedly the only agency with the power to investigate any and every government official engaging in bad behavior, is subordinate to the Inspector General (in that case, it is called the CIGIE, or the Council of the Inspectors General on Integrity and Efficiency) which supposedly, according to Wikipedia, "addresses integrity, economy, and effectiveness issues that transcend individual Government agencies; and increase the professionalism and effectiveness of personnel by developing policies, technical standards, and approaches to aid in the establishment of a well-trained and highly skilled workforce in the Office of Inspector General...CIGIE was established in October 2008 as an independent entity within the United States executive branch by the Inspector General Reform Act (IGRA)."

If anything, CIGIE was created as the veritable wolves, who guard the wolves, who guard the hen house.

To that end, any political party, oligarch, or plutocrat that captures the various Inspector Generals, in turn captures the entire direction of the United States of America.

There are Inspector Generals ("IGs") for all three branches of government, legislative, judicial, and executive, but within the IG community, there is no "separation of powers."

In fact, this is the massive illusion being perpetrated on the American people and the world - that in fact, the United States is NOT a government of "checks and balances," but rather a full blown dictatorship run by the Office of the Inspector General.

That might be one of the reasons that this term was stolen from Freemasonry lingo, wherein one of the symbols of Freemasonry is a Pyramid with a Capstone on top of it.

Because that's as high as you can go in this country to seek redress, remedies, or justice if you are getting ruined by the various corrupt and criminal government employees in the USA, from all 3 branches of government.

If one takes a look at these IGs, you will find that these people are all friends, and thick as thieves.

There is no diversity of opinion among them, and they never disagree or debate each other.

They are the ultimate arbiters of justice in this country, and boy, they are dirty.

So when are we as a nation, going to demand an audit and investigation of these Inspector Generals?

To find out if they are taking money and bribes, or sweetheart deals, or if they are ideologues, communists, NAZIs, racists, demagogues, activists, extremists, crazy, sexists, compromised by foreign countries, drug or alcohol addicts, or whatever other impairments which could result in catastrophe at the very top of the United States government.

The most amazing thing about this is that there is absolutely NO MEDIA coverage on the Office of the Inspector General, whether state or federal, with a full and virtual media blackout on their comings and goings.

And this needs to change, today, if this country is going to fulfil its promise of having a democracy and/or republican form of government, with checks and balances, and appeals, at every step of the way.

# Chapter 11

## *America Can Learn A Lot From Other Countries*

For all of the crowing on and on about how "America is Exceptional," and apparently can do no wrong, it sure has its fair share of social illness, dysfunction, redundancy, race problems, inefficiency, rampant stupidity, corruption, greed, filth, and other massive problems.

To that end, and if one has had the fortune to have been able to travel to many different countries and nations of the world, one quickly finds that the United States of America is not the end all, be all, and if its leaders and people would let go of their borne and bred arrogance and fear of the unknown, the country could actually improve and solve countless of its problems by incorporating and learning from the sometimes hard earned lessons of the rest of the words' people.

For example, the USA could learn a great deal about emulating the rigorous educational systems of both India and China, particularly with regard to science, mathematics, engineering and industriousness.

With regards to America's infrastructure problems, the US could look to Japan or even Northern Europe to see how subways and mass transit should run, with the superior engineering technology therein.

When it comes to cleanliness and order, any country in Europe will do, where the people and governments take great pride and care in personally maintaining their gardens, parks, train stations, streets, roads, sidewalks, countryside, urban areas, even buildings and arenas.

For some of the most crushing and devastating social plagues in America, such as rampant illegal drugs and narcotics use, the USA idiotically hands out hypodermic needles and lets drug addicts walk around like the living dead, zombie-like dangerous people threatening to children, families, and neighborhoods.

Why not follow the Iranian method, that is, incarcerating drug addicts not in prisons, but in forced detoxification facilities to be treated as a health crisis, weaned off drugs away from the mass population and the inevitable violence and crime that goes along with going cold turkey sober and being cut off from addictive drugs.

Many countries have some program like this, and sure, it could be viewed as a curtailment of certain civil liberties and human rights, but temporary separation from society has always been the punishment and consequence of anti-social, violent and dangerous behavior made even more exacerbated by the numbing effects of strong narcotics.

Every one know that Americans are generally obese, so why not emulate the active lifestyles, diets, and sports filled cultures of South America, Southern Europe, North Africa, and parts of the Middle East?

In other words, adopt and emulate the skinny healthy peoples' lives, diets and cultures.

The list of national strengths that could cure or improve American social illness is long and vast, but perhaps only a few at a time, or a handful at a sitting, could do wonders towards lifting the United States of America out of its generational malaise.

But first, in order to learn, open their collective minds, and heal/grow, America has to stop deluding itself, thinking that it's the best country and culture in the world, which it is clearly not.

# Chapter 12

## *Variety Is The Spice Of Life, But Extremism Is The Mouth That Burns*

Whatever your opinion of diversity or variety within the human species, whether you prefer as few differences as possible amongst a community, all the way to every other member of your society having noticeable differences whether physical, psychological or spiritual, the fact remains that every individual, and then consequently every society made up of those individuals, has a tipping point wherein they simply can not take it anymore, and begin to revolt.

Because human beings have no built in collective negative-feedback system, their communities and societies will keep transforming, changing, and expanding until the dominant or majority of those members say "uncle."

At that point, at best, political debates are had, and at worst, violence and cacophony result.

Neither side is theoretically wrong, or morally indefensible, but that community as a whole must then reach a consensus, engage in a dialogue, and come to a middle ground compromise in order for each and every member of that society to survive.

This is what is referred to as "Ordo Ab Chao," otherwise known as "Order Out Of Chaos."

This was also a mantra of Old European and early American colonial master establishments, so it is a deeply engraved value system of the Western societies.

This of course is the essential kernel of the clash by and between this Western bloc (now known as NATO and its sugar daddy, the USA) versus the deeply, religiously, and culturally entrenched (and now officially merged) Orthodox Christian Russian Federation, the deeply religious Islamic World, and the protectionist Asian countries using communism as a sword and a shield against sneaky and dangerous Western incursions, spies, terrorism, and other clandestine methods of sabotage and overthrow, that is the People's Republic of China, North Korea, and other combinations of all three (Indonesia, Malaysia, Singapore, Vietnam, Burma, and Laos).

Now many African nations, newly enriched by well educated native borne leaders who have returned from the vaunted universities of the West, as well as discoveries of their harnessing and controlling their own natural resources, have joined China and Russia because their memories of Western domination has been marked, understandably, by an extremely foul taste in their mouths, as well as distrust, disdain, rejection of their values (even the good ones), and even hatred, marred by organized slavery and colonialism beginning in the 1500s, followed through with countless acts of assassination, terrorism, disruption, sabotage, disorientation, and destruction through their European and Western militaries but mainly by their ultra secret, ultra insidious, sociopathic "intelligence services" which channeled hard cash, high tech weapons, and other temptations directly to rival tribal leaders of the same countries in order to keep them tearing each other apart, rather than focusing their ire and rage against their Western manipulators.

To that end, the current and final war currently being engaged in Ukraine is in fact World War III, and is expected to ebb and flow in intensity, but never truly be resolved until the last victor stands - and that victor will determine the course of humanity into eternity with regards to its religious, social, political, and existential value systems.

And the greatest lobbyers to this fight to the finish include, but are not limited to, extremist feminists, homosexuals, transgenders, islamic fighters, orthodox christians, white supremacists, jewish supremacists, pan-arabists, and conservative catholics.

These extremists are the only ones entirely committed to laying down their lives for the sake of securing a world wherein their "people" can live free, or die.

# Chapter 13

## *American Small Business Getting Crushed By Big Corporations And Government Funded Competitors*

In an every growing trend which has seemingly reached it Zenith in the last few years due to the global COVID pandemic, global government overreach moved by communist china and their teaming up with global oligarchs, and other government funded NGOs by the likes of billionaires like George Soros and leftists within the U.S. Government openly funding public services such as lawyers and doctors (and other professionals) to provide "support" and "services" to the masses (usually with very sub-par performance and professionals) the American small business is rapidly becoming as rare as seeing a unicorn in the forest.

Unfortunately the overwhelming and overpowering big businesses backed up and funded by the big banks and other financial institutions, with near limitless cash and bailouts even when the economy is under attack, or when the Federal Reserve decides to either raise or lower interest rates, increase or reduce monetary liquidity in the global market place, also tilts against small business owners who are then hit from the other side by left wing favored competition from government programs providing the exact same services at the tax payers expense (such as court appointed lawyers or government funded medical care, or whatever else).

The only democratizing force helping small business to survive, if not grow or prosper, has been the internet, with its enormous potential for rapid growth and community outreach through online advertising and global connectivity to customers (think Uber or Amazon), but even those avenues has been clamped down and the spigot shut off by the massive Big Tech media and social websites shutting down, canceling out, making disappear, or cutting off funding (see PayPal, other merchant service companies) to disfavored or "unhelpful" small business which challenge or threaten the oligarchs and plutocrats of today, with their sometimes sick and warped "value systems," such as forced trans-gender therapy on young children, extreme homosexuality, extreme abortion including past 9 months and after being birthed, racial and religious supremacy, pedophilia and child sex trafficking, illicit narcotics and recreational drug use, disarming the public so as not be able to protect themselves against tyranny, and other social sickness, wherein if you don't openly or actively support them, then you had better shut your mouth and opinion on them, lest you also be cut off from their financial systems, by their like-wise but extremely secretive perverts nestled within their "risk management" and "underwriting departments" enclosed within their financial institutions.

This is how creeping communism works, and the global oligarchs and global communists are actively meeting with each other, solidifying their grip on humanity, squeezing off small business and crushing individual freedom, to create a new world order, where you and your thoughts, don't even exist.

# Chapter 14

## *Big Tech Payment Systems Are Slowly Replacing The American Judiciary*

It used to be that when one party had a contractual dispute with another party over goods and services the 2 individuals would head towards their local courthouse and duke it out legally and equitably in front of lawyers and judges who had been trained for years, if not decades, in the subtle and complex intricacies of contract law and the uniform commercial code, complete with those professionals (usually doctors of law) who would draw upon their vast training and study into case law, statutory authority, legislative intent, treatises, other legal sources and hornbooks collected, analyzed, and collated over thousands of years to arrive at a competent, trustworthy, and fair written legal decision.

Now, with the advent of Big Tech payment systems, such as the imbeciles running the underwriting and risk departments over at PayPal, Stripe.com, Square, and other barely high school graduated mouth-breathers sitting at their desks, whole entire contracts in the tens of thousands of dollars, if not millions, are being decided on a whim and a lark by pimply faced morons with no education or training in the intricate complexities of contract law, and the results are very, very real.

One party has their money taken away, and another party is enriched somehow with either money, or product, or services, or all 3.

This paves the way for truly unfair results, implicit bias, racism, discrimination, revenge, retaliation, power trips, failure to understand english, cultural norms, hatred of certain classes of people, and other factors which should have absolutely no place in determining financial or contractual disputes whatsoever.

It was bad enough when Big Tech, following the trend by Big Corporations, started down the pathway of eliminating individual civil and human rights and constitutional guarantees by forcing any and all people who dealt with them (employees, customers, contractors) to sign an "arbitration agreement" which promised not to use the civil courts to resolve any or all disputes by and between themselves and the Big Corporation, thus quashing in the blink of an eye legitimate violations of law and human rights, but now this cancer has spread and metastasized into also applying the same arbitrary and capricious decision making in the financial transaction world as well, completely dispensing with courts of law, and replacing them with dark ages based thuggery and animal instincts to resolve legitimate financial disputes between credit card holders, banks, merchant services, and merchants/small businesses themselves.

Of course, the United States House and Senate Banking Committees remain fully and totally asleep at the wheel, unwilling to drag these wholesale abusers of law and contract back to the court rooms where they belong, while the judiciary simply rubberstamps these "arbitration agreements" without going to the actual merits of the cases at hand.

The United States of America judiciary and legal system slips further and further down the slippery slope into the Dark Ages, with the greedy billionaire global oligarchs of Big Tech and Big Corporations dragging its people along for the ride.

# Chapter 15

## *Organized Jews Are Planning To Leave America To Organized Blacks*

Unless you have been living under a rock for the past 5 years, it is quite obvious that as the Jews in the major cities are all packing up and getting ready to leave for Israel (well at least until Iran and their other enemies are neutralized) they are collectively preparing and leaving America's Blacks (preferably Prince Hall Freemasons) in charge of the major cities of American government.

That is, the executive, judicial and legislative branches of New York City, Los Angeles, Chicago and other major cities where currently Jews dominate the government.

Reason being, is that this was the deal struck by and between Jewish ANTIFA which was the communist brain behind the Black Lives Matter muscle that overtook and overcame the conservatives, christians, republicans, and other constitution law abiding American citizens in order to elect arch-organized criminal Joe Biden and his Irish Mob family to the Presidency.

Joe Biden has now repaid these ANTIFA/BLM thugs with key positions in the United States government, where they are now embarking on a massive pogrom of conservatives, christians, whites, republicans, libertarians, and anyone not literally sucking their toes and bending over backwards to kiss their ass.

There is no difference between Stalin's mass murder of "upstarts" in the former Soviet Union in terms of what kind of people the current Biden administration is going after, other than instead of killing them or sending them to Siberia on the spot, they are opting for neutralization by making people and dissidents disappear through "cancel culture," erasing them or minimizing them from social media, organized marginalization and ridicule, instructing American domestic and foreign intelligence agencies to infiltrate and push American judges, courts and their law clerks to harshly and without mercy target their enemies in state and federal court, and other methods of "soft kills."

This is the result of organized jewish communism and freemasonry's "evolution" into a more "humanitarian" organization, dispensing with the need to spill blood or kill off their enemies, when they can just, "turn them off" like one would switch off a radio or television set.

# Chapter 16

## *Global Communists And Global Oligarchs Have Made Civil Rights Violations Out Of Lifestyle Choices*

The only real threat to the complete and total grip on power by the already described merger by and between the Global Oligarchy and Global Communism, is the bringing of Civil Rights complaints and lawsuits by the masses, to the door of these merged tyrants.

That's why, in typical form, the Global Oligarchs/Communists (henceforth will be referred to as the "Global Control Freaks") have gaslighted humanity once again, and continue to stuff the "civil rights bag" with tons of inane, insane, wholly inappropriate, confusing, and often times dangerous social "choices" as "civil rights" violations as well.

To be clear, a civil rights violation is very clear to include issues traditionally viewed as discrimination and bias against minorities based solely on issues that they can not change, control, or that they were born with - phenotypical and genetic issues such as skin color, race, ethnicity, national origin, even gender (male and female please, none of these binary or countless other "artificial sexes") have always been used as definitions in nearly every single civil rights code drafted all around the world, since the dawn of civilization.

However, since the "slings and arrows" from the masses aimed at the global control freaks have been so effective when they are couched as civil rights violations in court or otherwise, the control freaks have now countered by "diluting" the pool of clear civil rights violations with countless "lifestyle choices," wherein the exerciser of those "rights" are making that choice completely and totally on their own, without the excuse or benefit of being able to claim that they are inherent to them or that they were born with.

Therefore, since the immense money power (billions) of the global oligarchs were instrumental in getting the American Psychiatric Association ("APA") to change their medical books and categorization of homosexual sex from "deviant" instead to a "normal and healthy lifestyle choice," the gates were flung open and the crack in the dam began to burst.

Very quickly other fringe groups made up of groups with "lifestyle choice" decisions began to follow the oligarch lobbying model, became organized, and started pumping with donation and election money into those political whores and prostitutes in the American (and European) legislature, executive, and even the judicial branch, immoral imbeciles who gladly took this money and slowly but surely began to include and dilute and swell with new legislation, the various categories of civil rights violations to include "lifestyle choices," such as homosexual sex, pedophilia, bestiality, BDSM, recreational narcotics use, transgenderism, satanism, and other social ills into their bag of tricks.

This of course angered traditional victims of civil rights violations, such as blacks, women, and other racial, ethnic, and darker skin colored minorities who could do nothing about the discriminated against quality that they were born with, and which were legitimately holding them back from societal progress, on a daily basis.

Then the various tax-exempt charitable 501c organizations ("civil rights NGOs") such as the American Civil Liberties Union ("ACLU") began to get flooded with massive financial donations from global oligarchs and communist organizations in order to transform them from the outside and inside, instead directing and gearing them towards fighting not racial, religious, skin color, or ethnic discrimination and bias by public and private organizations within society, wholly owned and controlled by them, but then using the vast majority of these civil rights NGOs human resources, money, clout, media power, and connections with U.S. government officials to aggressively push homosexuality, transgenderism, pedophilia, recreational narcotics use, and other social ills and deviant lifestyle choices into bona fide civil rights lawsuits, complaints, claims, and "struggles," while the traditional and aforementioned civil rights violations fell by the wayside, neglected, underfunded, ignored, diluted, disrespected, and swept under the proverbial rug.

Massive money (bribery) bought (and brought) this massive societal and global paradigm shift, by billionaire homosexual oligarchs over the past few decades such as Peter Thiel, David Geffen, Elton John, and scores of others who enjoy their "homosexual lifestyle choice," but are otherwise, rich, wealthy, powerful, politically connected white men, who just happen to enjoy sticking and sucking their dicks into other mens' mouths and anal canals.

"Civil Rights," these are most certainly not.

# Chapter 17

## *Humanity Needs To Ensure That Artificial Intelligence Is Also Programmed By Humanists, Not Just Control Freaks, Oligarchs, and Sociopaths*

Since Artificial Intelligence ("AI") is still a work in progress, generally thought to be in its infancy, it must be reiterated and stressed that all of humanity's betters must be allowed to infuse this burgeoning baby with their value systems as well, such as those value systems espousing, for example, the rules of the 10 Commandments for instance, or just basic common human decency.

Unfortunately, it seems that the greatest contributors to the body of data and knowledge (and this being the source for intelligent decisions becoming automated) appearing on the major television and media stations appear to be from cold hearted and analytical scientists, bloodless capitalists, communist and socialist demagogues, and others more interested in controlling and culling humanity, rather than seeing it thrive, develop, and grow.

To that end perhaps it would be a great idea to have others more interested in the propagation of humanity to have a seat at the AI programming table, rather than the emotionless and bloodless automatons that currently inhabit those chairs right now.

Religious figures, humanists, inspirational thinkers, and other philanthropists would be a good choice.

This way, if and when AI is forced to make a "tough decision" that could result in human death or harm, that it would instead choose the path of least casualty, rather than the path of least resistance, the latter of which appearing to be the favored choice of the various departments of defense, military, intelligence community, scientific community, oligarchs, plutocrats, communists, socialists, fascists, dictators, and other megalomaniacs.

Perhaps a common pool of value systems and knowledge could be compiled by today's leading humanists and philanthropists, that they could collectively agree on, in order to infuse their value systems and lists into the AI database at the ground floor of development, rather than trying to desperately put the genie back into the bottle years, or decades from now, after the world is covered in ash, smoke, and nuclear fallout because the assholes of humanity and their "value systems" won out, rather than the likes of the kinder elements of earth's global community.

Unfortunately, it seems that those proponents of AI are at direct philosophical odds with those who speak out against AI, those being the latter humanist and philanthropic community to begin with.

Therefore these humanists and philanthropists really should recognize the inevitability and bullying of those strong proponents of AI, and direct their energies towards the phrase "if you can not beat them, join them," that way, at least allowing their stamp of value systems being rolled up in, and programmed into, that vast body of data and source of artificial intelligence decision making, rather than being monopolized by the sociopaths of the modern age.

This is at least, something to think about.

# Chapter 18

## *Marjorie Taylor Greene Has Bigger Balls Than All Of Her Republican Male Colleagues Combined*

Right now the only united front against the outrageous and recently intrusive legislative and executive violations of the civil liberties, sense and sensibilities of ordinary Americans, is he one and only Congressional Representative Marjorie Taylor Greene.

This woman has bigger balls made of steel, in contrast to the rat-like cowards infesting the US House of Representatives and the US Senate, those bins full of cowardly, alcohol-soaked, bribery-laden, big tech/big media/oligarch beholden panty wastes, who are literally so compromised or so controlled by big money or big blackmail, that they are completely and totally immobile and neutered, standing in the corner, never daring to say or do anything that would offend their monetary gravy trains.

Their biggest nightmare which wakes them up in a cold sweat would probably be, "what if I lost the next election and had to get a real job?" rather than "what if my actions and omissions continued to lead the United States of America down the path of decline and destruction?"

The soul-less and ball-less congressmen and senators which inhabit Washington DC carefully choreograph and retain the services of video "sound-bite" companies to capture them briefly lambasting and/or bleating their faked and hyped up complaints directly at the faces of the various oppressors and abusers of the American people, such as FBI Director Christopher Wray, DHS Chief Alejandro Mayorkas, Education Secretary Randi Weingarten, and scores of others, but it all goes to naught when the camera lights go dark, while their videos live on YouTube into eternity with keywords designed to make them look heroic and patriotic.

Later on, those same recipients of their staged abuse swing by their offices on Capitol Hill with huge and massive checks and campaign donations to assuage their shakedown demands for more money in order to keep the bullshit charade going.

Only Marjorie Taylor Greene consistently, and perhaps Chip Roy, Rand Paul, and a few others, have the proverbial nutsac to continuously and verbally assault, offend, dress down, and legally and equitably smack around all of those vultures who are attacking the American people, whether from the public or private sector.

And for that, the American people thank her.

# Chapter 19

## *Rothschild's Affirmative Action Program*

Unless you have been living under a rock your whole life, and certainly over the last 30 years wherein the world wide web and its corresponding internet has been available to most of the global population, spreading previously and hitherto hidden, unknown, and secret knowledge, information, records, database, history and financial transactions for most if not all of the worlds' "movers and shakers," otherwise known as the global oligarchy or plutocracy, you will at once know the name of "Rothschild," or the "House of Rothschild."

You know, that man who famously invented the international banking system by planting his 5 sons in nearly all of the richest most important capitols of Europe, including but not limited to Paris France, London England, Frankfurt Germany, Vienna Austria, and Naples Italy.

There as history goes, a wealthy traveler could find his or her money ready and available (for a fee of course) waiting for him at any of these 5 destinations.

This idea was nothing short of simplistic genius, and it ushered in the age of the ATM Machine, Wire Transfers, and other electronic and physical modes of financial transfer (again, for a fee, of course).

This fee of course, is where the Rothschilds made their money, as "middle men."

After accumulating hordes of wealth through this method of not physically working, the Rothschild family began to realize that if they lent money to wealthy businessmen, and then kings, governments, and religious institutions, often on opposite sides of each other, then they could also make a financial "killing."

And so that story goes to the modern day, wherein some speculate that the Rothschild Family is valued at almost $3 Trillion Dollars if not more, making them the richest Oligarch (really Plutocrat) family in the world, creating and contributing to their investment businesses of choice, political contributions, crushing their enemies and competitors, while vaunting, supporting and lifting their favored chosen people, politicians, and businesses with interest free loans, grants, investments, seed money, angel investments, project finance, scholarships, and other methods of financial windfalls for their benefactors.

The Rothschild Family even built up the entire State of Israel with their massive wealth, and their name and mark is evident throughout the entire nation state in the middle east, as well as on all of their war crimes, institutional racism, death, and destruction.

So it comes as no surprise to make the next intellectual leap - that is, that some of the greatest, richest, most powerful, globally influential, and "surviving the competition" businesses and oligarchs owe their success, fame, fortune, and multiple financial rescue efforts to the "Rothschild Affirmative Action" program, because that's exactly what it is.

Many of these "successful" people, who facts prove are predominantly Ashkenazi (European origin) Jewish, sit at the forefront as CEO or leadership positions of some of the largest, most powerful, financially gargantuan companies in the world - in all industries such as Big Tech, Big Media, Big Finance, Big Pharma, Big Entertainment, and other "Big" international global business.

But if one actually gets to watch an interview with one of these "titans" in the business on say, YouTube or in any of the major media (they usually run from the media for good reason), one is usually struck at once, by how, on their face, these people are by and large, dumb as a box of rocks, can barely put a sentence together, provincial, have stupid looking faces, often have disgusting poor physical hygiene, are hideously ugly, don't know how to dress, are basically clueless as to how their own companies run (they notoriously rely on actual intelligent mainly third world people from India or China to run their day to day business operations, marketing, research and development, technical extrapolation and planning, and other areas designed to keep their products and companies head over heels over anyone else).

And if a smart, brilliant, ambitious competitor ("upstart") manages to eke past the hundreds of political, legal, logistical, financial, judicial, executive, legislative, military, and other illegal roadblocks that the Rothschild Financial Empire has managed to lay all around new and burgeoning business and ideas like land mines, then that company and its brilliant CEO is quickly targeted for either (1) absorption, or (2) destruction.

In other words, "join us or die."

The reason that this financial family is called an "Affirmative Action Plan," is because that is exactly what it is, taking people who otherwise would not qualify for success, money, investment, nurturing, training, education, cold hard cash, loans, grants, lawyers, etc to become successful and a "titan in their field, rather than actually having any real or recognizable talent.

And this is altogether unfair, and un-American.

# Chapter 20

## *The Use Of The Word "Woke" To Describe Annoying Abusers Of Equity Is The Ultimate Gaslight By The Deep State Oligarchy/Communists*

The fact that Big Media has taken to use the word "woke" to describe and define those people who frivolously or falsely claim victim hood status in an otherwise oppressive society on many levels and fronts is the ultimate "gaslighting" of those Americans (and people of the world) who legitimately can complain about being crushed under the wheels of the Global Oligarchy/Communist government merger currently taking place all over the world.

Ths truth of the matter is, being "woke," or "awake," SHOULD intuitively mean someone who has now become aware of, and cognizant to, the formerly hidden and invisible Deep State, their machinations and manipulations behind the scenes in order to further enrich and strengthen themselves at the expense of the worlds' people and masses.

To be "awake" when it comes to these Deep State criminal conspirators is obviously on its face, a GOOD THING, but Big Media (working hand in hand with Big Tech), which has been proven over the past 10 years to be funded and run by the Deep State, has made the term pejorative, negative, and insulting as a moniker.

This is classic "gaslighting," which the Merriam-Webster dictionary defines as "psychological manipulation of a person usually over an extended period of time that causes the victim to question the validity of their own thoughts, perception of reality, or memories and typically leads to confusion, loss of confidence and self-esteem, uncertainty of one's emotional or mental stability, and a dependency on the perpetrator."

In other words, the now mainstream use of the word "Woke" to describe people who analyze, point out, identify, and then share with their fellow human beings the hitherto hidden and criminal behavior of our global elites, is a successful psychological operation to make these people the new "conspiracy theorist," another nasty term which was actually discovered to have first been coined and introduced by, guess who?

The American Central Intelligence Agency, probably one of the largest components of the proverbial "Deep State."

So the next time you hear some dim-wit on the major media, or one of the many controlled politicians whoring themselves out to the Oligarchy as the "Peoples' Candidate" use that term to lambast and insult those heroic Americans and global citizenry who expose and publish such Deep State activity, think of this article, and recalibrate your opinion of that speaker.

www.ingramcontent.com/pod-product-compliance
Lightning Source LLC
Chambersburg PA
CBHW031548210526
45464CB00003B/1212